Day and

MW01269258

Contents

What Makes Day and Night?

The earth moves in a path around the sun.

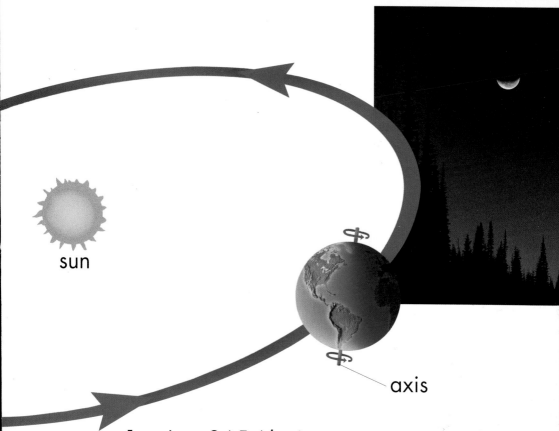

sun

axis

It takes 365 ¼ days, or one year,
for the earth to move around the sun.

Every day the earth spins
around once.
This makes night and day.
It is day on the side
of the earth
that faces the sun.

sun

day

It is night on the side that faces away from the sun.

sun

night

Day

U.S.

It is day on this side
of the earth.
People wake up.
They have breakfast
and get ready for their day.

Some people go to work.
Children go to school.

Some animals on this side
of the earth are awake too.

Birds sing and
bees buzz around.
Squirrels gather nuts.

Night

While the bees are buzzing
and people are working
on this side of the earth, something
different is happening halfway
around the world in India.

It is night there.
People climb into bed
and go to sleep.

Most of the animals there
go to sleep too.

But there are some
animals that wake up at night.
Owls hunt for food at night.
Crickets chirp.
Foxes and deer are awake
at night too.

The Earth Keeps Turning

Day turns into night and night turns into day. When the sun rises in India, it's time for people to wake up.

And halfway around the world,
in the United States,
it's time for people
to go to sleep.

And the Earth keeps spinning.

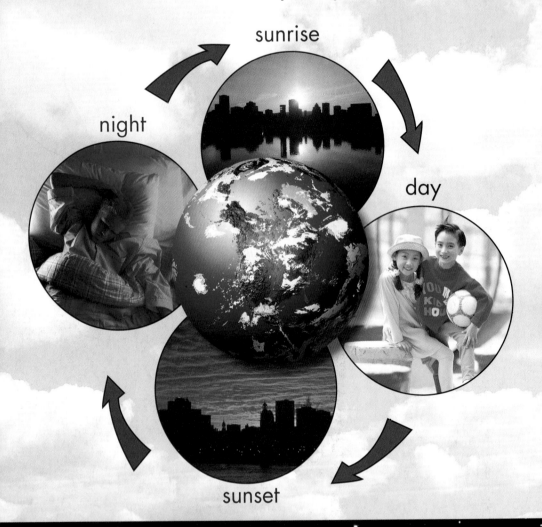

sunrise

night

day

sunset